A JOURNAL FOR
BAD
DAYS

A JOURNAL FOR

BAD DAYS

SELF-CARE STRATEGIES
to GET PRESENT WHEN
THINGS AREN'T PERFECT

EVELINE HELMINK

with Hilary Sheinbaum

SIMON ELEMENT

New York   London   Toronto   Sydney   New Delhi

SIMON
ELEMENT

An Imprint of Simon & Schuster, Inc.
1230 Avenue of the Americas
New York, NY 10020

First Simon Element trade paperback edition November 2023

SIMON ELEMENT is a trademark of Simon & Schuster, Inc.

For information about special discounts for bulk purchases, please contact Simon & Schuster Special Sales at 1-866-506-1949 or business@simonandschuster.com.

The Simon & Schuster Speakers Bureau can bring authors to your live event. For more information or to book an event, contact the Simon & Schuster Speakers Bureau at 1-866-248-3049 or visit our website at www.simonspeakers.com.

Interior design by Davina Mock-Maniscalco

Manufactured in the United States of America

10 9 8 7 6 5 4 3 2 1

Library of Congress Cataloging-in-Publication Data has been applied for.

ISBN 978-1-6680-2684-7
ISBN 978-1-6680-2685-4 (ebook)

Contents

A JOURNAL FOR
BAD
DAYS

Introduction

*Y*es, everyone has those really terrible, awful, shitty, very bad days. The upside? There are shortcuts to make these horrific days a little bit better—or at least allow you to step back and process and/or accept the rough bouts. *The Handbook for Bad Days* isn't a typical self-help book, and this *Journal for Bad Days* isn't either. There isn't a method or a multi-step plan to follow to eliminate bad days forever—just a number of questions to ponder while facing the worst days with courage, compassion, and your head held high. True happiness isn't about cutting out the bad days; it's about accepting life as it is—because it's often on those days, when everything falls apart, that we learn the most about what brings us comfort, resilience, courage, strength, and, yes, happiness. Within this journal, you'll find prompts to help you reflect on all of these topics and more.

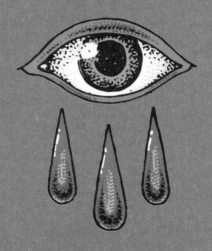

It's okay
TO NOT BE
OKAY

FOUNDATIONS

On Uncomfortable Feelings

On the outside, things aren't always what they seem. But even more often, when we have bad days, we don't know how to communicate with a vocabulary that describes what is wrong.

When was there a time you experienced a bad day but you couldn't verbalize what you were feeling? Did you describe your pain as a scene or give it a name? It might be a "feeling of being lost, when a sudden cold fog limits your sight and you can no longer see the forest for the trees" or a "weeping willow" moment. Has either happened for you? What did your bad day scene entail, or what is its name?

_____

_____

_____

_____

_____

_____

_____

_____

_____

_____

Calling Things by Their Names

These are the Five Great Emotions:

- Anger—when life feels unjust.

- Sadness—when life disappoints.

- Guilt—when you feel you're responsible for life going wrong.

- Fear—when, perhaps, there are bears on your road.

- Shame—when you don't seem to cut it.

Choose to focus on one, two, three, or four. Or write about all five. When were times you deeply felt this emotion? What happened? Who were you with? Where were you? What occurred leading up to this feeling? How often do you feel this emotion? What happens in your body when you feel this emotion rising? How was the feeling resolved?

_____

_____

_____

_____

Why It Is So Important to Fully Know Yourself

When someone asks me what the key to happiness is, I almost always give them the same answer: self-knowledge. Personal growth isn't always easy; sometimes that inward path or self-examination can be tough.

When was a time you learned a hard truth about yourself? What was it about, and what did you learn in the process? What changes did it inspire, if any? Alternatively, what personality traits did it make you proud of?

_____

_____

_____

_____

_____

_____

_____

_____

_____

_____

_____

_____

_____

You Could Call It Soul Hacking

Soul hacks are about letting go, flexibility, and self-knowledge. Where *life* hacking is for living efficiently, *soul* hacking is living to the fullest. Soul hacks offer tools so you won't get carried away as easily by misfortune. Whether it's deep-breathing exercises, venting to a friend, or going for a walk, only you can determine what soul hacks can make your life lighter and more meaningful.

What's a soul hack you utilize to ease anger, sadness, guilt, fear, and/or shame, or a combination of a few of these? How did you feel before? How did you feel after?

_____

_____

_____

_____

_____

_____

_____

_____

_____

_____

_____

Twelve Skills That Make Lesser Days Lighter

These skills aren't things like riding a bike or playing the piano. Nevertheless, they are important capabilities.

- Intuition—alertness to the subtle whispering and deeper knowing of your soul.

- Self-knowledge—knowing who you are and what moves you down to the darkest corners of your soul.

- Attention—being present to what is, as it is.

- Love—experiencing unconditional connection and unity.

- Surrender—the art of moving along with the flow of an uncompromising life.

- Resilience—a ladder for climbing out of deep wells and muddy pools.

- Strength—firm roots that keep you grounded and nourished.

- Compassion—love as a verb, love put into practice.

- Balance—a center, a core, from which everything originates and to which everything returns.

- Inner peace—a calm soul, even in a tempestuous outside world.

- Courage—the main ingredient for living a pure and true life through trial and error.

- Humor—the capacity to not take yourself and life so bloody seriously.

Of these twelve skills, which one is your go-to? Or do you employ several of these when you have a bad day? How did they help alleviate a less-than-perfect situation? What do you remember about those moments? Is there one skill you would like to develop? What would be a small step toward practicing that skill?

_____

_____

_____

_____

_____

Oh, and Don't Forget Your Body!

Not only can listening to your body alleviate bad days; in some cases, it can even prevent them from occurring at all. We can feel symptoms of very real stress in our head as migraines, brain fog, or pulsing aches. These signals can tell us to slow down, take it easy, or make a full stop.

What physical symptom (or symptoms) did you experience during stress, sadness, or a bad day in general? What was going on in your life or your day at the time? How did your physical symptom(s) feel at the moment? What helps you to release physical symptoms like those you describe? How does it change your course of action or your day's path?

_____

_____

_____

_____

_____

_____

_____

_____

_____

Help Me

The phrase "know thyself" is helpful in order to avoid bad days and rise up from them. But that doesn't mean you have to do it on your own. Support can be hard to accept, but needing someone to help you is perfectly normal, human, and acceptable.

On your bad days, who do you call for reinforcement? How do you know this person? How have they provided help in the past, whether through speaking words of affirmation, providing company, or simply serving as a sounding board on a bad day? What about them is comforting? Now that you're thinking about it, who else could you potentially ask for help?

_____

_____

_____

_____

_____

_____

_____

_____

_____

_____

Perfection *is a* MOVING TARGET

F*CK
WHAT MENTALLY
STRONG
PEOPLE DO

Manage the Mulling

Sometimes we worry, thinking the exact same thought ten thousand times, in a loop. But we can stop doing this. The best thing you can do is give your worries your full attention. Carve out space in your schedule.

Have you ever tried to make an appointment with yourself, just to worry? Was it helpful? How much time did you allow—fifteen minutes? An hour? Some period of time in between? Did you sit or take a walk to focus? How did it feel to dedicate uninterrupted time to letting your thoughts run wild? Can you also give yourself a boundary so that you wrap up at a chosen time?

_____

_____

_____

_____

_____

_____

_____

_____

_____

_____

The Flowers of Tomorrow Are in the Seeds of Today

Old habits can keep you trapped in unsatisfying patterns in your life, but establishing a routine can also have the opposite result: it can set you in motion.

What good habits have helped you on bad days, and how? What aspects of your current routine that are draining your energy might you let go of? Who or what would you be when you got rid of those habits?

_____

_____

_____

_____

_____

_____

_____

_____

_____

_____

_____

_____

_____

_____

_____

The Art of Kaizen

There is a Japanese philosophy, called *kaizen*, in which the path to change consists of teeny-tiny baby steps. A minute of meditation. Getting up five minutes earlier. One half glass less of soda. The result is the payoff and not an end in itself.

What baby steps have you taken, little by little, that have made a real change in your life? When did you start, and how has this habit evolved, whether it's stayed the same or become a bigger change overall? Is there something you'd like to achieve, and is there a small step you could take regularly to work toward that?

_____

_____

_____

_____

_____

_____

_____

_____

_____

_____

Laugh about It

Laughing causes you to take a deep breath. Your body is happy with laughter. When you laugh, the number of antibodies in your saliva increases, your muscles relax, your blood pressure drops, and you produce endorphins that work as an analgesic.

On a bad day, when was a time that laughing made things even just a little better? What did you laugh about? How did it bring levity, and perhaps a little mental relief, to the situation at hand? How can you re-create it?

_____

_____

_____

_____

_____

_____

_____

_____

_____

_____

_____

_____

Gratitude Feels Good

The sun is rising, and you are holding a fresh cup of tea—you can take it for granted, or you can also choose to be thankful for it. Considering what you have received makes you feel good, or at least makes you feel slightly better on a bad day.

What are you grateful for today? Write down three to five things that you are thankful for and how these things make your life more manageable.

_____

_____

_____

_____

_____

_____

_____

_____

_____

_____

_____

_____

_____

_____

Long Live Boredom

As an adult, you have so many fewer "in between" moments. There are hardly any moments when you have nothing to do. Being bored is not the same as meditation or rest, activities for which you make time and on which you focus your attention. When you're bored, there seems to be nothing worth your attention, nothing that gives you energy. With some patience, what is empty can fill up with reflection, daydreaming, creativity, or the simple acceptance that there is only nothing.

When was the last time you experienced boredom? Did you reflect on anything specific or think of something innovative? How did you feel during and after these moments of nothing to do and nowhere to be?

_____

_____

_____

_____

_____

_____

_____

_____

_____

Do the Savasana

Savasana is also known as corpse pose because you're lying there like a corpse—on your back, with no muscle tension, not doing anything at all. Except breathing, that is.

Try this at home, in your favorite room in the house. Lie on the floor and truly relax, allowing your thoughts and impressions to freely flutter without an active response. How did it feel? Did you try to make a to-do list or revisit thoughts—or let go? What would help you next time to let go more?

_____

_____

_____

_____

_____

_____

_____

_____

_____

_____

_____

_____

Loving-Kindness

Practicing loving-kindness isn't easy. In theory, it's beautiful; in practice, it can be difficult. Thankfully, it's a quality you can develop and adopt as your basic attitude.

Everyone has their particular flaws. When was the last time you realized this and, instead of snapping at someone (or yourself!), practiced loving-kindness instead? How did moving through negative energy to arrive at loving action make your day brighter?

_____

_____

_____

_____

_____

_____

_____

_____

_____

_____

_____

_____

_____

_____

WHAT are you trying to teach me?

YOUR LOVELY BODY AND BAD DAYS

Let's Talk about Sex for a Moment

We are sexual beings; sex is part of who we are. Yet sex is a vulnerable topic. Sex is good for your body, it's good for your energy, it's good for your soul. Sexual energy can prove to be a game changer for some on bad days.

Everyone has a different relationship with sex: what it means to them and how it makes them feel. What have you learned about your sexuality? Are you comfortable with yourself as a sexual being? Do you experience relaxation in relation to sex, and how could you enhance that?

_____

_____

_____

_____

_____

_____

_____

_____

_____

_____

_____

Sleep Is Sacred

Sometimes we just need to sleep it off. But, especially when your mind or body are super wired, it can be difficult to let go and surrender yourself to sleep.

What was the best sleep you ever had, and what happened leading up to it? Describe a perfect night's sleep. Where are you? What are you wearing? What rituals do you engage in before bed? What time do you go to bed? When do you wake up? What do you dream about?

_____

_____

_____

_____

_____

_____

_____

_____

_____

_____

_____

_____

_____

Tend to Your Bed

There are ways to devote attention to the place you sleep, to help you from feeling down even more on a bad day. Action items include:

- Investing in a quality mattress and nice bed linens.

- Making your bed in the morning.

- Making sure your bedroom is cool and well-ventilated.

- Leaving your electronic devices in another room.

- Not allowing screens in the bedroom.

Which (if any) of these practices do you follow? What's another bedtime routine (or two) that you do to maximize feeling better, and how do such routines make you feel on a bad day or in general? How do you feel if, by chance, you forget to complete a task, like turning on the AC or making your bed in the morning?

_____

_____

Why It's Better to Just Get Up

It's no fun waking up on bad days. Early-morning light is a balm for the soul. The morning carries the promise of "another day, another chance," and if you manage to tap into that, your day will take on a whole different kind of energy.

Building a routine in the morning will enable you to start the day slowly. What time do you get up in the morning? What would you like to get done in the morning, ideally? What would this mean for the rest of your day? How can you incorporate this intention in your routine?

_____

_____

_____

_____

_____

_____

_____

_____

_____

_____

_____

Take a Hot Shower

One of the most underestimated home remedies for mitigating a bad day is taking a hot shower. (You might have to come back to this prompt at a later time, FYI.)

The next time you take a shower, try this: Visualize washing off all your worries and seeing them disappear down the drain. Imagine all the negative energy that was hanging around you being scrubbed away.

After your hot shower, write how this practice made you feel, both physically and emotionally. What worries did you wash away? Can you describe or rate the difference between how you felt before and after your shower?

_____

_____

_____

_____

_____

_____

_____

_____

_____

_____

Crying Is a Form of Detoxing

Crying can be cathartic. There's a Jewish saying that what soap is to the body, tears are to the soul.

When was there a time you cried and felt cleansed in the hours or days that followed? What did you cry about? Where were you? How did you feel at the moment? What about the hours and days that followed? Do you feel better after talking with someone (a trusted friend or partner) when you cry, or do you prefer to process the emotions on your own?

_____

_____

_____

_____

_____

_____

_____

_____

_____

_____

_____

_____

_____

_____

_____

_____

_____

_____

_____

_____

_____

_____

_____

_____

_____

_____

_____

_____

_____

_____

_____

_____

_____

_____

_____

Once Around the Block

At times, walking is nothing more than shaking out that negative energy.

   If you walk, run, or hike, how often do you do it, and where? How do you feel in the moment and after? How does transporting yourself around (on your own feet!) give you time to think, decompress, or rid yourself of bad thoughts on a bad day?

_____

_____

_____

_____

_____

_____

_____

_____

_____

_____

_____

_____

_____

_____

_____

FOOD FOR THOUGHT

Giving Up *Is* an Option

Perseverance is important, but giving up doesn't always mean defeat, either. Sometimes you are liberating yourself from expectations and judgment.

Even if you had a moment of grief as you said goodbye to a dream or goal, when was a time you gave up on something and it was the right decision for you? Was the decision a quick one or premeditated? What happened that helped you start looking forward?

_____

_____

_____

_____

_____

_____

_____

_____

_____

_____

_____

_____

_____

_____

Advanced Complaining

Life will always find ways to be unkind to you. Once in a while, you need to vent.

What is something you want to vent about? What's bothering you or nagging at you, something that you want to get off your chest? Phone a friend or ask a housemate if you can have their ear. Or take a few pages in this journal and vent. Once you do, how do you feel? What did talking it out uncover for you?

_____

_____

_____

_____

_____

_____

_____

_____

_____

_____

_____

_____

_____

_____

Choice Overload

When it comes down to it, there are really only two choices: the ego choice and the soul choice. The difference is the feeling of tension and release. An ego choice feels hot, hasty, and impatient, while a soul choice feels grounded, wholesome, and truthful. An ego choice is an interpretation of what you feel, while a soul choice is rooted in knowing what you feel.

Do you recognize the difference between a choice made by your ego and a choice made by your soul? Can you describe them both and how they were different? What do you need to make soul choices? What do you already know when it comes to making soul choices? What do you need for that?

_____

_____

_____

_____

_____

_____

_____

_____

_____

#NoRegrets Should Be Banned

"I don't regret anything," some people say, or "Life's too short for regret." That's not necessarily the case for everyone—we're human, after all! But you can learn from your regret. Often, regret is no more than a hangover from a choice that wasn't right, something you denied or didn't allow yourself. Pema Chödrön said, "Nothing disappears until it has taught us what we need to know."

What is something you regret? How did regret feel? In your body? In your mind? What does this regret say about what you want for yourself? What have you learned from it? How have you made different choices since then?

_____

_____

_____

_____

_____

_____

_____

_____

_____

_____

Saying You're Sorry

There are a few elements to consider when you apologize to someone:

- Practice what you would like to say.

- Pick your moment.

- Be sincere.

- Apologize without expectations.

- Listen to what the other person has to say.

Based on a time when you apologized to someone, which of these elements were you most self-aware of before you apologized? What would make an apology acceptable and authentic when offered to you? How would the perfect sorry-sentence start?

_____

_____

_____

_____

_____

_____

_____

Perhaps a Coach After All

Getting help from an outside source can be productive, helpful, and meaningful to your future. That said, this person can't be a best friend or a partner, someone who has a bias or skin in the game. Nonjudgmental coaches can be extremely helpful on bad days.

Whether you have a coach or might be looking for one in the future: What subject, question, or theme would you share with someone who listens in an unbiased way? What you are not exploring now? What would you like to happen? What would you like to change about what's happening right now in your life?

_____

_____

_____

_____

_____

_____

_____

_____

_____

_____

Apologies and Forgiveness

Forgiveness comes in many shapes and sizes. Forgiving someone who didn't show up for your birthday party is of a different order from forgiving someone who severely breached your trust. Forgiving someone for doing something is not the same as saying you approve of it. Nobody is wholly good or bad through and through.

What is one thing you have forgiven someone for, or forgiven yourself for? What happened, and how did you come to accept forgiveness? Did it involve an apology? A confrontation? A deeper understanding of another perspective? What or who is still in the waiting room for your forgiveness? How would it feel to work on that?

_____

_____

_____

_____

_____

_____

_____

_____

_____

_____

does not have to
MAKE SENSE

THE
BIG BAD
WORLD
OUT THERE

Dealing with External Hassle

Wouldn't life be much easier if you weren't dealing with the big bad outside world? At some point, you have to transform anger to let it go.

Think about an imperfect, lesser day that you experienced. What could you have done to improve the situation for yourself? In hindsight, are your thoughts and feelings about what happened on that lesser day proportionate to what happened? What helpful skills that you have developed can you rely on when it comes to coping with these days?

_____

_____

_____

_____

_____

_____

_____

_____

_____

_____

_____

_____

And What Does This Say About You?

Especially on tough days, it can be a wise decision to close yourself off from other people's energy when the vibes aren't charging you positively. But it is certainly fascinating to ponder how you can use your interaction with other people as a crash course in self-knowledge.

Who is a person that has made you think deeply about yourself? What did you learn about yourself from your interaction with them? Did you practice self-compassion and kindness?

_____

_____

_____

_____

_____

_____

_____

_____

_____

_____

_____

The Lives You Don't Lead

Sonder is the realization that everyone is leading a life that is just as vivid and complex as your own—filled with their own ambitions, friends, routines, worries, and folly.

Realizing that can make us aware of our enormous emotional palette. What ambitions, friends, routines, worries, and folly do you possess that people don't likely know about you on the surface?

_____

_____

_____

_____

_____

_____

_____

_____

_____

_____

_____

_____

_____

_____

Social Media Detox

Social media is downright bad when things aren't going well for you. Everyone seems happier, more organized, fitter, younger, hipper, more successful, and smarter on the days when you don't feel that way about yourself.

When you consider getting back time spent on social media, what would you do instead? How do you feel doing these things you love, compared to binging photos and videos on social apps?

_____

_____

_____

_____

_____

_____

_____

_____

_____

_____

_____

_____

_____

_____

_____

Turn Off the News

News wakes you up, makes you alert, and gives you a sense of involvement and connection, but with what? Continuous news cycles trigger stress hormones, disrupt your concentration (and can in the long term even diminish it), and create noise in your day-to-day routine.

How do you feel while watching the news? Informed, stimulated, stressed, something else? Do you set limitations on how many minutes you will watch? And could you pare back your news sources to three quality networks/platforms/papers? Instead of bad news, what are some things you could watch or do to occupy your time?

_____

_____

_____

_____

_____

_____

_____

_____

_____

_____

_____

What's Your Panic Room?

If you're not feeling good on the inside, it's comforting to be in a safe and soul-soothing environment.

Where is a space that you feel your safest? Is it a place that's quiet? Is it in a hotel lobby, in the car in traffic? Write a list of places where you feel you can escape to find your inner calm, and why you feel at peace there.

_____

_____

_____

_____

_____

_____

_____

_____

_____

_____

_____

_____

_____

_____

_____

The Emergency List

The same way you keep a list of numbers hanging on your basement door or shoved in a kitchen drawer, maintain a running list of activities that make you feel good. Some examples: sleeping, meditating, writing, and exercise.

What are activities that make you feel your best on good days and can help with the bad? What do they entail, where do you do them, and how long do you participate?

_____

_____

_____

_____

_____

_____

_____

_____

_____

_____

_____

_____

EVERYDAY LIGHT THINGS

Playing Creator

We're used to being in our heads; that's where society encourages us to be. But do you know what's good for your soul? To create. Especially on the hard days. Working with your hands will lighten your days, because it adds to your sense of self-worth and autonomy.

What's something you create or have created with your hands? Do you feel present in the process, and if so, what are you focused on in those moments? Imagine yourself in a workshop space with every imaginable tool and all the supplies you need. What would you pick, and what would you make?

_____

_____

_____

_____

_____

_____

_____

_____

_____

_____

Write It Out of Your System

It probably has become clear to you that it isn't always productive to just let yourself marinate on a bad day. Writing is a powerful way to express yourself, and when you write, you translate a bad day into concrete words. You alleviate the traffic in your head by "parking" your thoughts in a different spot than your own mind.

In the morning, fill this page with anything that comes up in your mind, whether you have inspiration or not. Need some help? Set a timer, choose a genre or form, start with a question or a standard opening, or write a letter to your younger self.

_____

_____

_____

_____

_____

_____

_____

_____

_____

_____

_____

_____

_____

_____

_____

_____

_____

_____

_____

_____

_____

_____

_____

_____

_____

_____

_____

_____

_____

_____

_____

_____

_____

_____

_____

The Consolation Cardigan

We know that touch has a comforting effect for adults as well as kids. And an object—specifically a fluffy or soft one—can create comfort and/or security.

What is something you own that creates comfort in your life, especially on a bad day? A blanket? A childhood stuffed animal? What does it look like? What does it feel like, and how does that make you feel? When did you get it, or who/where did you get it from? What does it remind you of?

_____

_____

_____

_____

_____

_____

_____

_____

_____

_____

_____

_____

Because You're Worth It

Material goods don't make you happy, but at the same time, having nice things can contribute to your happiness. Keep the nice, good, quality things! Just don't surround yourself with subpar stuff, because it will give you a subpar feeling.

Look around you. What things actually take energy away from you feeling light, clean, and happy? Which of your belongings would you be relieved to not see or use again?

_____

_____

_____

_____

_____

_____

_____

_____

_____

_____

_____

_____

Fake It Till You Make It

In other words, bluff your way to your goal. Perhaps you know that your circumstances aren't right yet, but your brain will remember the feelings you gave yourself: pride, satisfaction, self-confidence.

When was a time you faked it until you made it? How did it feel to exhibit these positive—if faux—emotions, and turn them into real, genuine ones in the end? Think of a future goal. What would your future self want you to channel into reality?

_____

_____

_____

_____

_____

_____

_____

_____

_____

_____

_____

_____

_____

_____

_____

Radio Mantras

Mantras can be "lullabies for the soul." When reciting mantras, you chant words of wisdom that help you calm your soul, vibrate off negative thoughts, and bring positive intentions into the world. The mantras don't have to be highly intellectual or "officially" spiritual to have meaning.

What is a mantra you've used or are using now? It can be something you've read, heard, or adopted over time. It could be something you made up yourself. How does this mantra make you feel? What does it inspire you to do—whether that be calming down, pushing forward, or feeling better on bad days?

_____

_____

_____

_____

_____

_____

_____

_____

_____

_____

_____

Create Soundtracks for Your Life

Music is a language that transcends boundaries—both those separating the people of the world and the one between you and the highest heaven. Music lends everything color, meaning, atmosphere, and emotion. Music is healing.

What song or songs have great meaning for you and hit you differently than most—and how do they make you feel? What is your go-to song for a cry or for tough times? Or a song you like for big, celebratory moments? What are some songs that are soul-soothing, with calm, chill, relaxed vibes, or that help you get energy out of your system?

_____

_____

_____

_____

_____

_____

_____

_____

_____

Art Is Good for You

Even the most trivial anxieties can be a source of creation and transformation. Art challenges you to form an opinion about what you find beautiful and what you don't, to be open-minded, to see how creative and expressive your mind is. And art is always truthful. Experiencing art can be uplifting and, at the very least, provide a moment of quiet.

Whether it was visiting a museum, observing an art installation, admiring graffiti, or some other artful expression—what was it that moved you? How did it distract you from your feelings or inspire new thoughts, or take you to a different place entirely?

_____

_____

_____

_____

_____

_____

_____

_____

_____

_____

LOOK
AROUND
FOR A
MOMENT

Nature Is a Mirror

Once you become aware of all the things going on around you in nature, you have one of the most comprehensive educations you can find. Everything has its rhythm. There's a period of growth, of bloom, of withering, and of stillness.

How have you mirrored nature? When was a period of growth for you? Bloom? Withering? Stillness? What did you experience during these times, and what did you learn? In your personal lifle, what season would you say you're in now? The space of winter, the celebration of summer, the excitement and thawing of spring, or the new start of fall?

_____

_____

_____

_____

_____

_____

_____

_____

_____

_____

Landmarks Along the Way

A landmark is a visual reminder of good times and bad times, and of how those two keep occurring, one after the other, over and over again. It could be a building, a tree, a view, or anything else.

What landmark serves as a reminder to measure your state of mind? How often do you pass it? Does it change shape with time, look different to you depending on the season or your mood? How have you reflected similarly or dissimilarly when you pass it by?

_____

_____

_____

_____

_____

_____

_____

_____

_____

_____

_____

_____

_____

Go Watch the Waves

On bad days, go to the ocean. If nothing else, look at it on YouTube. Or listen to an "ocean sounds" soundtrack.

When you are in, by, or listening to the water, where are you? Describe the setting—is it the ocean? A stream? A swimming pool? A bath? Even just thinking about these things, how does your mind feel? Calmed, comforted, distracted, or something else entirely? How does your body feel? How about after?

_____

_____

_____

_____

_____

_____

_____

_____

_____

_____

_____

_____

_____

_____

THE SOUL
KNOWS BEST

A TAD ESOTERIC, BUT THEY DO HELP

Synchronicity: Hints from the Universe

Your intuition doesn't scream, she whispers. She's subtle, funny, mysterious, and demands attention in the most wonderful ways. Depth psychologist Carder Stout describes synchronicities as "incidents of spiritual significance that ask us to momentarily dampen our self-obsession and consider the possibility of the divine." Wow.

When was a time that something so coincidental, so in sync, happened to you? Describe how it happened, where you were, what you felt. Did everything feel in balance or off, caused by a spark, or completely natural? Through which senses does your intuition speak to you?

_____

_____

_____

_____

_____

_____

_____

_____

_____

_____

On Dreaming

You can think of the cycling of day and night as an hourglass that you keep turning over. The day flows into the night and vice versa. Likewise, you can start to see your dreams as conversations with yourself. Your dreams show you what's going on, in a free-flowing, creative, and, at times, bizarre form. Call them the messages from your unconsciousness.

What places, people, or themes do you often dream about? What do they represent for you? What was a dream you remember? When was it, and what was it about? How did it clarify your emotions and inner thoughts?

_____

_____

_____

_____

_____

_____

_____

_____

_____

_____

About Your Inner Child

A theme that is closely related to the inner child is innocence—big, not-knowing, unfettered curiosity, lightness, and security. That's your deepest core. Our need for play doesn't stop when we reach adulthood. Playing isn't a guilty pleasure; it should have a natural place in your life.

How did you play when you were a child? When was the last time you played or goofed around or discovered something new as an adult? What are some ways you can play today, tomorrow, or in the future that will support the lightness of your inner child?

_____

_____

_____

_____

_____

_____

_____

_____

_____

_____

_____

_____

Create Your Own Rituals

Making the mundane valuable—that's what rituals can do for you on lesser days. Your life will become more meaningful because of them. Rituals don't have to be epic and riveting.

What are some rituals or tasks that you do every day? On lesser days, how do they help you stick to a plan or a schedule so you can move throughout your day? What is your favorite daily ritual, and how does it benefit you, even if it's something mundane?

_____

_____

_____

_____

_____

_____

_____

_____

_____

_____

_____

Muttering a Prayer

Praying is being in conversation: articulating your question, expressing your doubts, asking for help and forgiveness. This can be addressed to whoever or whatever feels sincere to you, whether that is God, a higher power, the universe, earth, love, or anything else.

What's a time you prayed and felt relief and gave something that worries you to an anonymous address in the cosmos. What did you pray for? Did you feel grateful, thankful, or a mix of emotions? What would you like to give from your hands to the higher powers now? How does knowing that you can surrender your worries make you feel?

_____

_____

_____

_____

_____

_____

_____

_____

_____

_____

Create a Home Altar

A home altar is a simple way to connect with something outside yourself, whether it be divine, a cosmic energy, or the cycle of life. It can be wonderfully comforting on bad days, and creating one isn't complicated. Whether it's in a hallway, a corner of a bedroom, or anywhere else, you can garnish it with cherished objects, maybe fresh flowers—and you're all set.

What does your physical altar, or the one you envision for yourself, look like? Where is it, and what objects are present? How can you represent your past, present, and future in this space? Are they gifts from others or items you made and purchased independently? How do these things make you feel, and how did you select each?

_____

_____

_____

_____

_____

_____

_____

_____

Living in the Present

"Living in the now" is an often-heard adage in spiritual circles. Being in the moment, the now, can really put your troubles in perspective, give you comfort and air. On a lesser day, you might actually want to book a one-way ticket to a place far away from this fabled "now," because the present moment is painful or for any negative reason. But our minds will swing from past to future to present.

The key lesson of living in the now is flowing along with life as it is. What from the past pulls you back from the now? What in the future pulls you out of the now? What brings you back here?

_____

_____

_____

_____

_____

_____

_____

_____

_____

_____

Moon Inspiration

There are four periods for the moon:

- New Moon—time to let go and start over.

- First Quarter—time for courage, change, and manifestation.

- Full Moon—time of abundance and harvesting what you have sown.

- Third Quarter—time for clarity, choices, forgiveness.

If you were the moon, what cycle do you identify with now? Where will you go next?

_____

_____

_____

_____

_____

_____

_____

_____

_____

_____

Wabi-sabi

Wabi-sabi is an ideal that offers an alternative to the perfectionist mindset. It represents the essence of life. *Wabi* refers to simplicity, stillness, and elegance. *Sabi* is the beauty that comes with age: cracks, rust, or moss. There are three truths in wabi-sabi:

- Nothing is permanent.

- Nothing is ever finished.

- Nothing is perfect.

How have you celebrated your imperfection? How does it make you who you are? And on a bad day, what do the three truths of wabi-sabi inspire?

_____

_____

_____

_____

_____

_____

_____

_____

_____

About the Authors

*E*veline Helmink is a journalist and writer living in Amsterdam. She is editor in chief at the international media brand Happinez, which shares insights and inspiration for personal growth and a meaningful life. She is the internationally published author of *The Handbook for Bad Days* and *When a Loved One Has Dementia: A Comforting Companion for Friends and Family*. Besides her work in the media and publishing fields, Eveline works one-on-one with clients as a licensed Master Coach Practitioner. She navigates topics such as meaningfulness, change, acceptance, and leadership. Eveline is also known as a presenter of sold-out live events in the Netherlands, featuring guests such as Esther Perel, Cheryl Strayed, and Nicole LePera (@theholisticpsychologist). Follow Eveline on Instagram @Eveline.Helmink.

Hilary Sheinbaum is a journalist covering food and beverage, health and fitness, beauty and lifestyle, entertainment, weddings, and more. Her trend and profile pieces have appeared in the *New York Times*, *USA TODAY*, *Marie Claire*, *Travel + Leisure*, and *AM New York*, as well as on the *Today* show, Yahoo!, and many other outlets. Hilary has been featured as an entertainment and lifestyle expert on *Inside Edition*, CBS, *Fox & Friends*, and more. The former South Floridian graduated from the University of Florida and currently lives in New York City.